To find out more about

management systems, check out:

LMS Success!

A STEP-BY-STEP GUIDE TO LEARNING MANAGEMENT SYSTEM ADMINISTRATION

For videos that supplement this book, check out YouTube channel Learn Tech Collective.

www.YouTube.com/LearnTechCollective

In addition to the Learn Tech Collective YouTube channel, there are even more resources available to those who purchase the book and join Learn Tech Collective.

TO REGISTER YOUR BOOK, GO HERE:

Bit.Ly/LearnTechCollective

(CASE SENSITIVE)

You will receive an email directing you to videos and written resources that relate to this book. You will also be able to post responses to book activities and ask for advice in a private LinkedIn group. (If you don't have a LinkedIn account, you will need to create one to access this resource.)

You will be able to access all associated resources, for free, for 90 days. If you wish to continue your access after 90 days, you will have the option to pay a small monthly subscription fee. This fee supports the development of new content.

The author and the members of the private LinkedIn group will support you as you learn more about learning technology! This book is offered in print and e-book formats from:

www.Amazon.com

And other retailers

The LMS Selection Checklist

Katrina Marie Baker

Resources of Fun Learning

Los Angeles

2018

Published by Resources of Fun Learning
Copyright © 2018 by Katrina Marie Baker
All Rights Reserved
ISBN 978-0-9862469-3-7

A BIG THANK YOU...

This first thank you is to you, the reader, because you are part of the learning technology industry. We are in a field that grows and changes constantly. It can be hard to keep up at times, but we get to help people learn every single day. We are part of something beautiful.

My sincerest appreciation goes to everyone who helped fund my crowdfunding campaign. You made it possible to republish this book and *LMS Success!* Your names are listed on the Supporters page near the back of the book. It was important to me that I would be able to publish this second edition without giving up control of the content to a publisher. Thanks to you, I was able to turn down a major literary contract and follow my heart on the approach to both books.

As with all of my writing, this book is dedicated to my Mom and Dad, and my Grandma. I love you.

Thank you also to Tracie Marie Cantu, my editor, mentor, and sassy voice of reason. And to Kent Russell, for your endless patience and serenity. You would make an awesome LMS administrator.

Finally, love to everyone who says hello on social media or participates in my classes. Especially when my classes are at 8AM.

CONTENTS

INTRODUCTION

HI THERE!

It's nice to meet you, LMS knowledge seeker. Given the title of this book, you are probably looking for a new learning management system and would like to know what details you should consider and what questions to ask. Maybe you would like to know more about the features of an LMS, and how such a system can help your organization. If so, this is the right book for you.

The contents of this book are perfect for training managers, LMS administrators, and other corporate folks who want a simple breakdown of what an LMS can do.

If you would like a more comprehensive look at learning management system administration, please check out the mother of this book, *LMS Success!* It's available on Amazon from the same author, Katrina Baker.

THE SECOND EDITION COMES WITH NIFTY TOOLS...

The LMS Selection Checklist was originally published in 2015, and it was the first book that provided a comprehensive list of LMS features. This second edition is special because, in addition to the updated written content, this book gives you access to tons of FREE online resources that will help you during your LMS journey. For details, check out the first pages of this book.

There is a YouTube channel of videos, a selection of documents that save you time, and a private LinkedIn group so that you can post responses to the questions asked in this book. You can also use the group to ask your deepest LMS questions and get help from other administrators! Even if you never thought you'd be a learning technologist, we will help you become one.

"WHERE CAN I FIND THE SUPPLEMENTAL RESOURCES?"

To receive your supplemental resources, all you need to do is join Learn Tech Collective. Check out the first page of this book for instructions.

After registration, you will receive an email with a link to a private LinkedIn group just for readers of this book. This group gives you the ability to post responses to book activities and ask questions of fellow LMS administrators. You will also be directed to "unlisted" YouTube videos that are only visible to members of the private LinkedIn group, and documents that make it easier to complete certain LMS tasks.

"DO I NEED TO BE A TECHIE TO READ THIS BOOK?"

NO! Very little technical knowledge is required. There are a few areas where you are asked to consult your IT department because the topic is advanced, or your organization may have specific policies that will affect decision-making.

Speaking of IT, your IT department should be involved in your LMS search. Networking, security, authentication... If these areas are not your professional focus, it is always best to ask the pros for their opinions.

"HOW DO I USE THIS BOOK?"

If you flip through, you'll see the book is divided into nine chapters, with a few sections per chapter. Sections contain lists of LMS selection criteria, presented in question form.

If you are about to start interviewing LMS vendors, have a seat with this book and its resources. Watch some of the Learn Tech Collective videos, check out articles within the Learn Tech Collective LinkedIn group, or read some of *LMS Success!* Ask questions in the private LinkedIn group. Get an idea of the overall usefulness of an LMS and how the selection and implementation process works.

To get started, you'll need to ask a cross-section of your organization how they plan to use the LMS. Include representatives from all departments in this discussion. Using this book as a starting point, brainstorm 30 or 40 features that you wish to have in the LMS, then assign a priority level to each of these features. If you would like a template to assemble your LMS requirements list, one is available to members of Learn Tech Collective. There is also a video explaining how to use the document.

Once you are finished creating your requirements list, you can use it to ask vendors questions during their product demos. If desired, send your requirements list to a few vendors that are strong contenders, and create a side by side comparison of which vendors can offer you which features. (There's a template available for this too!)

This book can also be used to create a more formal exploratory document, known as a Request for Proposal (RFP). You might be familiar with these if you work with a government entity or large corporation. You can provide an RFP to a prospective vendor, and include a list of LMS features you require. Ask your procurement department if there is an RFP template you should use.

"DOES THIS BOOK TELL ME EVERYTHING ABOUT MY LMS?"

Nope! This book is here to get you started with your LMS vendor selection process. Throughout the book, we will discuss questions and issues you should address in greater detail with prospective vendors.

"OKAY, MYSTERIOUS BOOK WRITER... WHO ARE YOU?"

I'm Kat. I wrote this book because I love learning management systems. You may think I'm crazy since you're probably buried in the details of buying your new system. It gets more peaceful once you have a functional LMS.

I'm known in learning and development for my work as a consultant, speaker, and author. I love learning technology so much that I've implemented or administered nearly thirty platforms. Learning management systems have taught me a great deal – most of all a sense of humor, which I hope to use throughout this book and its resources.

If there is one thing that sets me apart from other authors and analysts in this industry, it's that I don't participate in corporate referral programs or sponsorships in exchange for endorsements. I only talk about products that I personally use and find to be helpful.

WHAT IS A LEARNING MANAGEMENT SYSTEM (LMS)?

An LMS is a server or cloud-based software that allows you to plan, implement, and assess learning in many forms. Learning management systems make it possible to deliver training content in many formats, monitor course participation, and assess student performance. A well designed LMS will reduce the amount of time you spend on administrative tasks associated with training. It will also make it easy for learners to find resources and track their progress.

There are many LMS features that help you engage learners, such as gamification, social learning, and web conferencing integrations. An LMS can be as simple or complex as your company wants it to be.

Besides learning management systems, there are other types of learning technology platforms out there. For example, you may have heard of a Learning Content Management System (LCMS) or Learning Record Store (LRS). If you would like to learn more about these, check out the YouTube channel Learn Tech Collective. View the video *Learning Technology Defined: The Difference Between an LMS, LCMS, and LRS.*

Now, let's go through some criteria to select your new LMS.

1

CATALOGS, COURSES & SESSIONS

An easy-to-use course catalog is the backbone of every great LMS. The quality of your courses and sessions is important, but if a user can't find learning content, we have a problem!

Ensuring a smooth experience for users is important, and we're not just talking about the learners. Instructors and administrators will constantly manage your organization's courses and sessions. Having the right course and session management tools will keep everyone happy and working efficiently.

MANAGING THE COURSE CATALOG

Many organizations have hundreds or even thousands of course catalog items! As you can imagine, the course catalog will become messy very quickly if you don't define some standards for your administrators.

Decide what course fields you want to utilize when creating courses. For example, if you want every course to include a course description, duration, and category, set that expectation for your administrators. Be specific in your instructions. Define how long a course description should be, and what information it should include. Define that the course duration should always be tracked in hours, or in minutes.

Think about how the learner will search for content. What information will make it easy for a learner to find courses that interest them? How can you use course categories, filters, and other catalog features to make searches simple for the learner?

Finally, consider what time-saving tools the LMS provides to help you manage the catalog. For example, if you ever decide to change the entire structure of your training program, you will definitely appreciate being able to make changes to a batch of courses.

If you have questions about anything you read in the following sections, post in Learn Tech Collective's private LinkedIn group. Instructions to join can be found in the front of the book.

#1 Within the course catalog, do course listings have standard attributes, such as course description, duration, and categories?

#2 How easy is it to enter and revise catalog information?

#3 Can hyperlinks be included in the catalog's course descriptions?

#4 How easy is it to specify where to display a course in the catalog?

#5 Can a course be included in multiple catalog categories?

#6 How easy is it to make mass changes to the course catalog? For instance, if you wanted to rearrange your course categories and the corresponding courses, could you upload a spreadsheet of your changes?

#7 Can a course or course session be hidden from the users' view, without being deleted from the LMS?

#8 Can an instructor set a course to be automatically hidden from the course catalog after a particular date? For example, if an instructor knows that materials for a compliance course will be out-of-date on January 1st of next year, the course may be automatically hidden on December 31st.

#9   Can an instructor-led course be temporarily hidden from the catalog if an appropriate course instructor is unavailable?

#10   Is it possible to include materials hosted externally (such as YouTube videos) as courses in the catalog?

#11   Once logged onto the LMS, how will users access the course catalog?

#12   Can a user search the course catalog by keyword and title?

#13   How easy is it for users to navigate, search for, and launch/register for courses?

#14   Is it possible to generate a printable version of the LMS course catalog?

#15   Can the entire course catalog be exported? This can be helpful when you transition to another LMS.

#16   Does your organization have additional criteria?

BUILDING & UPLOADING COURSES

Learning management systems are brilliant at tracking and delivering content, but in many cases, that's not all they do. Some platforms actually help you build and store the content you provide to the learner. Pretty nifty, right? But using built-in course development tools can be good or bad. Let's say you change learning management systems in a few years. Will you be able to use the content you built in your current LMS? It's a good question to ask of your vendor.

As you read this section, if you wonder what a course number is, it's a number that uniquely identifies a course. It can be a random number generated by the LMS ("COURSE 168953") or it can be a manually entered number that an administrator defines ("FRANCE COMPLIANCE 001 2018"). Yes, a course number can often contain letters! Some organizations really care about being able to manually define course numbers because it helps them keep their catalog organized. There are lot of ways to organize a catalog, so whether you use manually entered course numbers entirely depends on your workflow.

If you are new to the world of SCORM, AICC, and xAPI, you are not alone. There's more information about these protocols in the book LMS Success! Feel free to post any questions you may have in the Learn Tech Collective LinkedIn group.

As a final note, be sure to have prospective LMS vendors show you the process you will use to upload different kinds of course content. Your administrators will be doing this constantly!

#17   Does the LMS include a built-in content management system?

#18   Does the LMS offer built-in course authoring software?

#19   Does the LMS have podcast or webinar management tools?

#20   How simple is it to add, modify, or delete an existing online course? Have the vendor demonstrate.

#21   What about an instructor-led course? Again, have the vendor demonstrate.

#22 How easy is it for multiple instructors or administrators to participate in the creation of a course?

#23 Are there safeguards against accidentally deleting a course?

#24 If a course is accidentally deleted, can it be restored?

#25 Can courses and sessions be copied to create blank courses and sessions?

#26 Can you choose which features of an existing course or session to copy into a blank course or session?

#27 Can course numbers be chosen and assigned manually by instructors or administrators?

#28 Can course numbers be automatically generated by the LMS?

#29 Can an instructor include a facilitator guide with course materials, visible to other instructors, but hidden from class attendees?

#30   Can an instructor choose a provided template, or upload a template, for certificates of course completion?

#31   Can all elements of a course be spell checked by the instructor?

#32   Can PowerPoints be embedded or uploaded directly into the LMS?

#33   Does the LMS support 3D simulations?

#34   If your organization uses third-party content from vendors such as Skillsoft, does the LMS offer vendor-specific tools that will speed up the course upload process?

#35   Does the LMS accept video and audio uploads in multiple formats?

#36   Does the LMS support HTML5 courses? HTML5 courses are viewable on mobile devices.

#37   Does the LMS accept courses that conform to common protocols? Common protocols include: SCORM 1.2 | SCORM 2004 | AICC | xAPI / Experience API | Other desired protocols

#38   Does your organization have additional criteria?

MANAGING COURSES & SESSIONS

How do you make it easy for your instructors to easily deliver course content? An LMS should save them time, and it can actually reduce stress throughout your organization.

For example, let's say supervisors are frustrated when their employees sign up for classes and don't notify them. Some learning management systems allow you to automatically email a supervisor when one of their employees has registered for a class. You can also set certain classes to require supervisor approval before an employee can enroll.

Do you have trouble managing class sizes so that you can fit everyone in the room you reserved? Do you have attendees register or drop classes five minutes ahead of the class start time, causing you to scramble and adjust at the last minute? There are LMS features in this section that may appeal to you!

#39 How easy is it for an instructor to assemble an online or instructor-led course within the LMS, without administrator assistance?

#40 If instructor-led classes are offered on a predictable schedule, can recurring sessions be created based on a class template?

#41 Can multiple instructors manage a class session?

#42 If an instructor updates course material in the LMS, is it possible to store an archived copy of the previous course material?

#43 How easy is it for an instructor to manage when registration opens and closes for an instructor-led session?

#44 Is it possible to require instructor approval before a user can enroll in a class session?

#45 Can instructors specify a class size and waitlist size for instructor-led sessions?

#46 Can users be required to successfully complete a course prerequisite before viewing an online course, or registering for an instructor-led session?

#47 Can an instructor waive a required course prerequisite?

#48 Can an instructor override the class size entered for a given session and allow more users to enroll?

#49 Is it possible for an instructor to manually update a class roster? For example, if a class registrant does not show up to an instructor-led class, the instructor could remove the registrant from the roster.

#50 If a user fails to attend a class session, can the instructor record the absence using one of multiple attendance statuses? Statuses may include No Show or Cancelled.

#51 How easy is it for an instructor to assign grades and give feedback on assignments?

#52 Can grades be imported and exported between Excel and the LMS grade book?

#53 Can instructors see how much progress class attendees have made? For instance, can instructors pull a report that lists the percentage of course completion for each participant?

#54 Does the LMS automatically record the date and time that users launch online course material?

#55 Is it simple to specify deadlines for course completion?

#56 Can a course be assigned without a deadline?

#57 Is it possible for an instructor to set a deadline for specific course elements?

#58 Can the instructor limit the amount of time a user can spend on an assessment or course element?

#59 Do the dates and times associated with class sessions automatically adjust based on the user's time zone?

#60 Can a specific class session be hidden from public view, or restricted to specific LMS users?

#61 Can session enrollment be restricted to users who are within a specified geographic area?

#62 Is it possible to cancel a class session and reregister attendees for a different session?

#63 Can a user unregister from a class without instructor assistance?

#64 If a formerly withdrawn student reenrolls in a course, is it possible to recover the student's records for that course?

#65 Is it possible to search for instructor-led sessions by using multiple search parameters (e.g., location, instructor, subject category, etc.)?

#66 Is it possible to have users complete a pre-assessment and automatically assign courses based on assessment results?

#67 Can users be required to complete a survey after finishing an online course? How about an instructor-led session?

#68 Does the LMS provide a way to display a list of instructors to users?

#69 Does the instructor list include contact information, classes taught, credentials, and/or a biography?

#70 Can instructors external to your organization be included in the instructor list?

#71 Does your organization have additional criteria?

2

TALKING, TESTING & REPORTING

Some learners have a pretty dark perception of online courses... Sitting in their home office, all alone, with no instructor to help with questions. In reality, a good LMS will help instructors and learners communicate in a variety of meaningful ways.

In addition to communication, your LMS will likely play a major role in the delivery of assessments, and the reporting of user learning activities. Learning management systems are ideally suited to both tasks and offer a broad range of robust tools to make testing and tracking more efficient.

ANNOUNCEMENTS & NOTIFICATIONS

An instructor can spend hours making sure learners are aware of class changes, upcoming deadlines, and new learning resources. The good news is, an LMS can automate many of these administrative tasks! Consider the types of notifications listed in this section. Which of these would save your organization time?

#72   Is there an area on the homepage where you can include company announcements and news?

#73   Can the LMS homepage include a Twitter feed, stock quotes, or company news videos?

#74   Can the LMS deliver course-specific announcements?

#75   Can an instructor set automatic email reminders to remind users of upcoming instructor-led sessions, assignment deadlines, and overdue materials?

#76   If an instructor changes the time or location of a class session, will the LMS send a notification to all affected attendees?

#77   Is it possible to archive or otherwise save announcements given during a specific course session for later reference?

#78   Can announcements be edited after their initial release?

#79   Is it possible to send announcements via text message using the LMS? For example, if an instructor cancels a class session with short notice, he/she could notify attendees by text.

#80   Can your organization use the LMS to release emergency notifications to all users?

#81   Can automatic email confirmations be sent when a user enrolls in a class, waitlists a class, requests to register, or cancels registration?

#82   What other automatic reminders can the LMS send?

#83   If a user cancels enrollment in a class, is a notification automatically sent to his/her supervisor?

#84   Can your organization modify the LMS templates for email confirmations?

#85   Is it possible to deliver optional, supplemental materials for both online and instructor-led courses via links that are included in automated emails?

#86   Does the LMS generate and send calendar appointments for class sessions and other deadlines?

#87   Is it possible to sync the LMS course calendar with Microsoft Outlook calendars?

#88   What tools does the LMS offer to assist in promoting, delivering, and tracking attendance for webinars and podcasts?

#89   Does your organization have additional criteria?

COMMUNICATING & SUBMITTING ASSIGNMENTS

When delivering online courses, it's especially important that the learner feel connected to their instructor. If the learner doesn't feel they can communicate effectively, they can feel isolated and lose interest in the class. As you look through this section, consider what ways your learners will want to communicate with your instructors. Also consider whether your learners will submit assignments, and if so, in what format.

#90   What methods can a user employ to ask questions of an instructor, in either an e-learning or virtual instructor-led course? Is it easy for users to communicate with the instructor?

#91   Can a user deliver an assignment or ask a question via audio file?

#92   Can an instructor answer user questions via audio file?

#93   Can audio and text be exchanged privately between two users, or a user and an instructor?

#94   Is it possible for a user to have a live chat with their instructor, either privately or with a group of fellow students?

#95 What moderator tools does the LMS offer for chats, webinars, podcasts, and discussion forums?

#96 Can users upload assignments to the LMS via a dropbox?

#97 What file formats can be uploaded by users as part of their assignments?

#98 What is the file size limit for assignments submitted to the LMS dropbox?

#99 Are there tools available to assist instructors in grading group assignments?

#100 How easy is it for a user to view their grades, and how much detail is provided?

#101 If the LMS will deliver compliance courses or other materials required by law, can completion of said courses be communicated to your organization's HRIS or other system of record?

#102 Does your organization have additional criteria?

ASSESSMENTS & SURVEYS

Assessments and surveys may be an important part of your organization's training program. Many LMS vendors provide built-in tools to help you create and deliver these items. When you are creating content using built-in tools, be aware that you may not be able to take that content with you should you choose to transition to a new LMS someday. If you want to go the safe route, use an e-learning development tool, such as Adobe Captivate or Articulate Storyline, to build your content.

If you have questions, check out Learn Tech Collective's private LinkedIn group. Instructions to join can be found in the front of the book.

#103 Does the LMS have a built-in assessment building tool?

#104 Does the LMS have a built-in survey building tool?

#105 Can the LMS send a course evaluation form to users following a completed course? Following completion, can this form be sent to an LMS administrator, or another designated party other than the instructor?

#106   Can assessments and surveys be completed on a mobile device?

#107   If the LMS has an assessment building tool, does it accommodate all of the question types your organization needs? These may include: Multiple choice | True/false | Matching | Essay | Fill in the blank

#108   If a question is multiple choice, can the order of multiple choice answers be randomized?

#109   Can the order of questions be randomized automatically by the LMS?

#110   Does the LMS accommodate a question bank or quiz bank? A quiz bank allows the questions that appear on an assessment to be randomized. If fifty questions are in the quiz bank and an assessment is twenty questions long, the LMS will pull twenty questions randomly from the bank.

#111   Can questions be copied from one assessment to another using a quiz bank?

#112   Can assessments be copied from one course session to another?

#113 Can essay questions be graded online using the LMS assessment tool?

#114 Can users view instructor feedback on their essay questions?

#115 Does the LMS assessment tool allow users to include mathematical symbols in their answers?

#116 Can an assessment supply feedback to users based on correct or incorrect answers?

#117 Can assessments be automatically graded by the LMS based on criteria specified by the instructor?

#118 For question types that are automatically graded, such as multiple choice, are users able to view a grade immediately?

#119 Is it possible for a user to automatically receive recommendations for courses to review, based on assessment results?

#120 What tools does the LMS provide to assist in the tracking of proctored exams? Is there a way to record the proctor's identification information, completion date, and other associated information?

#121 Is it possible to set up an assessment so that a proctor password is required in order to launch?

#122 Does the LMS allow the browser to be locked during assessments so that additional browser windows cannot be opened?

#123 Does the LMS allow your organization to define the devices able to access assessments? This is often done by restricting the IP addresses that are able to access content.

#124 Can assessments be set to automatically appear to, or be hidden from, users on a specified date?

#125 Can assessments be released to select groups based on date and time, user ID, completed assignments or courses, or a combination of these criteria?

#126 How easy is it for an instructor to view when a user completed an assessment?

#127 Can an instructor view how long a user spent answering a particular question?

#128 Can an instructor restrict how many times an assessment can be attempted?

#129   Can assessments also be set so users are allowed
an unlimited number of attempts?

#130   Does your organization have additional criteria?

REPORTING

Learning management systems are great at tracking course completion! Many LMS vendors offer highly customizable reports that allow you to dig into your learners' retention rates, learning preferences, and professional development needs. Some of these reports are even displayed as colorful bar graphs and charts, which definitely makes analytics more fun for everyone.

Consider who should receive reports, and how often. Some LMSs can automatically send reports on a recurring basis to specified users.

#131   What standard reports are included with the LMS? Are they customizable?

#132   If your organization is customizing the LMS to include custom user or course fields, can those custom fields be included in reports?

#133   Ask the vendor to show you which properties of a course are trackable within the LMS. Are there properties that your organization wants to track that the vendor does not list?

#134   To what extent can reports be filtered to produce the data your organization would like to see?

#135   Can an administrator or instructor schedule a report to automatically run at a later time?

#136   If reports can be scheduled, can reports be run on a recurring basis?

#137   Can scheduled reports be emailed to a user? To a group of users?

#138   Can reports be viewed directly in a web browser?

#139 Can a report be sorted alphabetically or chronologically directly in the browser, without exporting?

#140 Can report data be subtotaled in the browser, without exporting?

#141 Can reports be printed directly from the LMS without being exported first?

#142 In what formats can reports be exported?

#143 Can supervisors pull reports that contain data pertaining to their subordinates?

#144 Can an administrator build a new report and share it with a group of users they specify?

#145 If you are linking to content on the Internet, is the LMS capable of reporting completion of that content?

#146 Does your organization have additional criteria?

REPORTS YOUR ORGANIZATION MAY WANT

Your LMS will be able to run a variety of reports. Some will appeal to administrators, and others will appeal to supervisors or learners.

For example, an administrator may want a report that tells them how many people started a particular course during the past week. Or the administrator may want to see how many hours of content learners have consumed within a particular timeframe.

An instructor may want a report that shows how a group of learners performed on a particular e-learning assessment question, to make sure that question made sense to the learners. They might also like a report of how many people have registered for next week's classes.

A supervisor may want a report that tells them who on their team took classes this quarter. And a learner may want to automatically receive a copy of their transcript every month.

What kinds of reports would benefit your organization?

#147 Scores for assessments and courses

#148 User answers to individual questions from assessments and surveys

#149 Number of attempts, and duration of user attempts, for assessments

#150 User's full transcript, so he or she can save or print it

#151 Course completion status by user

#152 Attendance by course and by user

#153 A list of modules within courses

#154 Sessions offered, by course

#155 Schedule of classes along with venues and training resources/equipment

#156 Course registrants, by session

#157 Number of continuing education units associated with each course

#158 List of licenses and certifications achieved by users

#159 User attendance of instructor-led courses and sessions

#160 User enrollment cancellations

#161 User progress within a course or learning track/curriculum

#162 LMS logons

#163 Course logons

#164 What other reports would you like?

3

LEARNING TRACKS & ALL THAT JAZZ

Learning tracks, also known as curricula, allow you to group courses based on a variety of criteria, such as subject or level of difficulty. Each course group can be equipped with rules so that users are automatically assigned new courses as they complete content within the learning track. What a time saver!

You can even associate groups of courses with a skill or competency, assign groups of skills to each job role within your organization, and ensure that each role is assigned a custom curriculum that will cultivate the right skills. Continuing education units, which are legally required for some fields of work, are also trackable.

LEARNING TRACKS & CURRICULA

Learning tracks are all about organization. Bundling a group of courses together in a track means you can assign the entire group as a single unit, which saves you administrative time. You can also make sure the learner takes courses in a specific order, so they receive more basic content before moving along to more advanced concepts.

#165   Can courses be organized into learning tracks or curricula easily? Have the vendor demonstrate.

#166   Can learning tracks be automatically assigned to users based on criteria you specify? For example, can you automatically assign a group of courses to new students or employees?

#167   How easy is it to make a group of courses mandatory for a group of users? What is the difference (if any) between the delivery of a mandatory course and a non-mandatory course?

#168   Is it possible to create a deadline that affects all courses within a curriculum or learning track?

#169   Can an administrator create user groups with defined attributes? If so, what attributes can be used?

#170   Can user groups be used by administrators to assign courses or learning tracks?

#171   Can user groups be used to pull reports related to courses or learning tracks?

#172   Does your organization have additional criteria?

SKILLS & COMPETENCIES

There are likely certain skills or competencies you would like to cultivate in your learner base. For instance, you might want to support the development of leadership skills, effective communication, supply chain management, or financial accounting. Some learning management systems offer you the ability to associate skills and competencies with the courses that support their development. This is commonly referred to as a competency-based learning platform.

If you have questions, check out Learn Tech Collective's private LinkedIn group. Instructions to join can be found in the front of the book.

#173   Is it possible to associate a group of courses with a particular competency or skill, and then assign multiple competencies or skills to a job role? This would potentially help your organization create a targeted curriculum for each role.

#174   Can your organization's job descriptions be imported into the LMS?

#175   Can uploaded job descriptions be associated with skills or competencies?

#176   Can a user search for a curriculum of courses intended specifically for their job role?

#177   Will the LMS allow users to complete ungraded self-assessments that assess existing skills and recommend appropriate courses?

#178   Can individual development plans be built by a user, or by a supervisor on a user's behalf?

#179   Can development plans for a user be shared with other supervisors?

#180   What assessment methods are available to assist in identifying skill gaps?

#181   How easy is it to automatically assign courses that are appropriate to a user's skill level, based on previous assessments?

#182   Is it possible to search for users who have a particular skill or competency?

#183   How easy is it to compare skills and competencies required for different positions within your organization?

#184   Is it easy to create, modify, and delete curricula/learning tracks, and competency/skill sets? Have the vendor demonstrate these tasks.

#185   Does your organization have additional criteria?

CONTINUING EDUCATION UNITS (CEU)

If your industry requires continuing education units, there is great news! A learning management system can save you tons of time administering, tracking, and reporting required learning activities.

#186   Does the LMS offer built-in continuing education (CE) tracking tools for your organization's industry? Such credits are common in fields such as medicine, accounting, and law.

#187 If certifications are part of your organization's curriculum, does the LMS have any specialized certification tracking features?

#188 Can continuing education units be added to courses?

#189 Is it possible to track continuing education credits that fall into different compliance categories?

#190 How easy is it for a user to search for CEU-eligible courses within the catalog?

#191 Can you set a maximum number of credits that a user can accumulate in a specific CEU category?

#192 Can automatic reminders be set so that users remember to complete a certain number of continuing education credits by the respective deadline(s)?

#193 Can an administrator set a user to be excluded from reminders and notifications regarding a specific continuing education requirement?

#194 Can continuing education rules or policies be displayed for users to view?

#195   Does your organization have additional criteria?

4

FEELING SUPPORTED

Do you feel the love? Many LMS vendors offer extensive training for your instructors and administrators, which can greatly help your organization adjust to a new system. And customer support has gotten so much more creative in the past couple of years! Be sure to explore the clever methods LMS vendors offer to help you, help your users.

TRAINING FOR USERS & ADMINISTRATORS

Things can get hectic when you're in the late stages of your LMS implementation. Your LMS vendor may be able to help by offering training sessions, videos, tip sheets, and marketing materials that will spread the word about your LMS. If your learners haven't seen a learning management system before, you'll want to tell them all about its benefits in addition to explaining how to navigate the interface.

As for your administrators, they will need an in depth understanding of the LMS and any tasks associated with their role. Training often takes days for super administrators! Definitely allot time for your administrators to become proficient in the LMS, and during contract negotiations with your LMS vendor, try to get administrator training thrown in for free. It can easily save you a few thousand dollars.

#196 What training is provided by the vendor to your organization free of charge?

#197 Is training offered by the vendor for your organization's LMS administrator team?

#198 Will the vendor assist your organization's administrator team in training end users?

#199 Can training be delivered by the vendor at your company's location?

#200 Are online training seminars available?

#201 Will training be offered on a periodic or as-needed basis?

#202 Is training documentation provided by the vendor? Materials may include a manual, tip sheets on how to do common tasks, and basic guides for end users.

#203 If training documentation is provided, can you modify it to include your organization's branding?

#204 Is training documentation limited to print materials, or are video tutorials and simulations provided?

#205 Does your organization have additional criteria?

CUSTOMER SUPPORT

It's so important to make sure your LMS vendor can provide the level of support your organization needs. Some vendors are based in other countries and keep business hours that are consistent with their time zone. Decide ahead of time whether that will work for you and adjust your list of prospective vendors if needed. Keep in mind that vendors sometimes offer different service packages, meaning a vendor may provide your organization with 24/7/365 service for an extra fee.

#206   What types of customer support are available? For example, can users IM, email, and call the vendor? Is support just for administrators, or for users as well?

#207   If the LMS vendor is based in a different time zone and only works standard business hours, how will that affect your organization?

#208   If your organization's employees speak multiple languages, will customer support be offered in multiple languages?

#209   Many vendors offer customer support that may include directly accessing user accounts or course content. Does the vendor offer this? Is it a security concern for your organization?

#210   Do you want the vendor to be able to alter user settings during help sessions? Are they capable of doing so?

#211   From your organization's perspective, how are support tickets viewed and tracked? Is there an online portal available to track your customer support cases?

#212   How extensive is the vendor's "frequently asked questions" section for users? For administrators?

#213   Are there mouseover tips available to explain different buttons on the user interface?

#214   Does your organization have additional criteria?

USER INTERFACE SUPPORT FEATURES

It's always nice to be able to offer users just-in-time support the moment they get lost! Some learning management systems provide built-in tools so a user can access help directly from the user interface. This saves both the user and your LMS administrators time.

#215 If the LMS requires users to manually log on, can users request a forgotten password?

#216 Can a user "rescue" their forgotten password by answering security questions?

#217 Is there a "Help" icon available to users that displays basic troubleshooting information?

#218 Can the help articles available to users be modified to better address your organization's customized interface?

#219 Is live technical support available to users by phone or chat?

#220 When a new user logs onto the LMS for the first time, are they offered a "new user tutorial" to introduce them to basic LMS features?

#221 Does your organization have additional criteria?

5

INTERFACES & HOW TO USE THEM

Now we're getting fancy. For our purposes, the LMS interface includes all areas of the system visible to a given user. Many systems offer ways to make the interface reflect your organization's look and feel. And the customization fun doesn't just affect the end user! There are many ways to assemble custom user profiles with different levels of administrator or supervisory functions.

CUSTOMIZING THE USER INTERFACE

You want learners to feel at home in your learning management system. And what better way to do that than to match the platform to your organization's branding? Many LMS vendors offer their clients the ability to customize the LMS by changing the appearance of the platform to suit different groups of learners.

#222 Can the LMS user interface be customized with your organization's colors?

#223 Can your organization's logo be added?

#224 How about custom banners and icons?

#225 Is it possible to reorder or delete tabs, menus, and other methods of navigation?

#226 Can the text associated with menus, tabs, and other interface features be changed for all users? For example, you may want to change a tab to read "My Team Members" instead of "My Employees."

#227 Can an administrator create custom page headers and footers for navigation within courses?

#228 Is it possible to have multiple themes for different groups within your organization? For example, you may want your German office to have an interface in the German language. Or you may want the IT team's theme to display different colors and logos than the Marketing team's interface.

#229 Can a user personalize his/her own interface by changing, reordering, or deleting elements? Some systems allow users to drag and drop page elements, on the homepage, for example, to suit their needs.

#230 Can the LMS vendor's name be removed from all pages?

#231 Is it possible to use a customized domain, or URL, for your LMS? In other words, the LMS may have the URL OurOrganization.org/LMS instead of LMSVendor.com/YourOrganization.

#232 Does your organization have additional criteria?

COURSES & SESSIONS FROM THE USER PERSPECTIVE

Do not, I repeat, do not choose a learning management system without walking through the interface from a user's perspective. It is absolutely critical that a learner be able to search for and launch a course easily, with as few clicks as possible. There is nothing worse than spending five minutes searching for a five-minute video! Also, make sure a learner is able to launch a course by clicking a hyperlink contained in an email. There is a significant number of vendors who don't make it easy to link directly to course content, and many organizations need that functionality.

#233 How easy is it for a user to launch an online course?

#234 How simple is it to navigate an online course?

#235 Is there a calendar of instructor-led courses available to users? Sortable by location, topic, and date?

#236 Can users self-register for upcoming instructor-led courses?

#237 Are users able to bookmark their place in the course materials?

#238 Can a user delete a course from their assignments list that has been assigned by an administrator or supervisor?

#239 If a user can delete assigned courses, can he/she also restore deleted courses, so they can be accessed again?

#240 Can a user add learning records for non-company training, such as licenses issued by a third party?

#241 Can users print certificates after successful completion of a course or program?

#242 Can users manually modify their time zone within the LMS?

#243 Is it possible for a user to participate in a class session while remaining anonymous to other participants?

#244 Does your organization have additional criteria?

COURSES & SESSIONS FROM THE ADMIN PERSPECTIVE

All administrators appreciate having a clean interface where they can efficiently create courses and sessions. But you can have a lot more than that! Some learning management systems have special tools that make it faster to complete routine administrative tasks. Do you think your admins would appreciate having some of the features listed in this section?

By the way, if you have lots of administrators, definitely ask prospective LMS vendors about creating multiple system roles. You don't want to give many people the permissions necessary to harm your precious course catalog. Is it possible to create multiple levels of administrators with different system roles?

#245 Can an administrator have permissions to affect only one domain of the LMS or only one group of courses?

#246 Can an administrator create a course workflow or template, to help instructors organize course materials?

#247 Can you limit permissions to create course templates to a select group of administrators?

#248 Can an administrator add custom fields to the LMS? Is this done with or without help from the LMS vendor?

#249 Can an administrator easily import and export a user's learning history?

#250 Can new users be added using a manual batch upload process?

#251 Is it possible for an administrator to track when a user last accessed the LMS as a whole or a specific course?

#252 Does your organization have additional criteria?

THE SUPERVISOR INTERFACE

Supervisors can really benefit from the tools an LMS offers. It's so important to keep track of an employee's development and provide continuous learning opportunities, and it's great to be able to check out a learner's transcript when it comes time for evaluations and promotions. If supervisors are happy with your LMS, they'll help you advertise it to their employees, which means the system will benefit your organization even more.

#253 How are employees associated with their supervisor? Is this information automatically provided to the LMS by your organization's HRIS?

#254 Can supervisors view their team's course completion progress through a special dashboard?

#255 How useful are the reporting tools provided to supervisors?

#256 Can an administrator manually assign employees to a supervisor?

#257 Can an administrator temporarily change who employees report to if a supervisor takes an extended absence?

#258 Can a supervisor view courses currently assigned to their reports?

#259 Can a supervisor assign an online or instructor-led course to their reports?

#260 Can courses be set to require supervisor approval before a user is officially registered?

#261 Can a supervisor confirm the completion of on-the-job training and provide course completion credit without an administrator's help?

#262 Can supervisors use the LMS to send messages to their direct reports?

#263 Can a supervisor assign training and run reports that include indirect reports?

#264 Does your organization have additional criteria?

6

SOCIALIZING THE LMS

Did you know your LMS could be a social media site? The new wave of learning management systems encourages fun interaction between users. Learners can play games together, rate course content, and read each other's social profiles. And they can do it all from their mobile devices! Go ahead and pick out your profile picture. You know you want to.

SOCIAL FUNCTIONALITY

Employees often enjoy learning with others, as opposed to learning alone in front of their computer. If a learner is able to ask questions of peers, comment on courses, and share advice within the LMS, it will become a gathering place. Courses become the beginning of a development experience where employees are able to learn from each other by sharing experiences and best practices.

#265 Can users create an LMS user profile, similar to a LinkedIn or Facebook profile?

#266 Can blogs be maintained by users and instructors within the LMS?

#267 What about wiki pages for different subjects or courses, created by instructors?

#268 Is there a WYSIWYG or HTML editor available to edit blog, wiki, email, and/or discussion forum content?

#269 Can users rate course content?

#270 Can users filter the catalog by course ranking and/or popularity?

#271 Does the LMS integrate with social media platforms? Examples include: Facebook | Twitter | YouTube

#272 Does the LMS support discussion forums?

#273 Does the LMS accommodate threaded discussions?

#274 What moderator tools are available for the discussion forums?

#275 Is it possible to restrict posting so that the instructor must approve a post before it is visible?

#276 Can users post anonymously to discussion forums?

#277 Can users have private discussions that are hidden from the instructor's view?

#278 Can discussion forums be shown or hidden by the instructor?

#279 Is it possible to password-protect a discussion forum?

#280   Can an instructor assign a grade to a user's discussion post?

#281   Can an instructor create multiple discussion forums associated with one course, so that class attendees can work together in small groups?

#282   Can documents be attached to discussion posts? What file formats are allowed?

#283   Can users embed links in discussion posts?

#284   Can a user run a search for content within the discussion forums only?

#285   Does your organization have additional criteria?

GAMIFICATION

While we're all here, why don't we play a game? Friendly competition is a great way to encourage employees to continuously access the learning management system. Just remember, in order for gamification to work, "winning" has to actually mean something. It's not enough to provide learners with points or badges, or a ranking on a leaderboard. Provide recognition or rewards that are meaningful to employees who choose to play.

#286 Does the LMS offer a leaderboard, showing the top scores of users within a specific game?

#287 Where does the leaderboard appear? On the LMS homepage?

#288 Is the LMS capable of running multiple games for multiple user groups at the same time?

#289 Can a user participate in multiple games at a given time?

#290 As part of a game, can a user be required to complete a given group of courses?

#291 Is it possible to base a user's game progress strictly on how many courses or how many training hours they have completed?

#292 Can a user earn incentive or reward points by completing game elements by a particular date, or by achieving a certain score within a course?

#293 Can users earn badges that can be displayed on their LMS profile? Badges may be issued for completing a course, reaching a milestone, or achieving a rank on the game leaderboard.

#294 Can supervisors manually award badges to their employees?

#295 Can your organization upload custom badge designs?

#296 Does the LMS come with generic badges?

#297 How can a user track their game progress and evaluate performance?

#298 Does your organization have additional criteria?

MOBILE

If your workforce works remotely or is constantly on the move, you may want to make sure they can access training content from their mobile devices. It isn't enough for your e-learning content to be designed for a mobile environment. Your learning management system also needs to be responsively designed in order for learners to have a good mobile experience.

#299 Can users view the LMS with their mobile devices, using a browser? Be sure to test the system's functionality yourself, on multiple devices.

#300 Is the LMS interface easily viewable on both smartphones and tablets?

#301 What mobile devices are not compatible with the LMS?

#302 What browsers are not compatible with the LMS?

#303 Does the LMS come with a native application for mobile devices? If so, users can access the LMS by tapping an icon on their device, rather than accessing their browser and typing in the LMS site address.

#304 Can your organization brand the app with your logo and colors?

#305 If the LMS can be accessed via an app, is the app available for user download from iTunes, Google Play, the Windows store, etc.?

#306 Can assessments and surveys be completed through both a mobile browser and app?

#307 What other types of content are viewable?

#308 Consider your existing training content. How much of your organization's training content would be viewable on a mobile device?

#309 Is online/offline synchronization available? This functionality makes it possible to download course content to a mobile device whenever the Internet is available. The content can then be completed even if the device can't access the Internet. The user's course completion will be relayed to the

LMS whenever the device reconnects to the Internet.

#310 Can a user or administrator access LMS reports on a mobile device? Are the reports easy to read?

#311 Can an instructor or supervisor access tools specific to their function using the app?

#312 Are there any major differences in functionality between the web version of the LMS, and the app version?

#313 Does your organization have additional criteria?

7

PROTECTING THE LMS

You knew we would get here eventually. An LMS stores data and requires system maintenance, and there are security and authentication details to work out. Oh my.

It actually isn't so bad taken bit by bit, with the help of some nice folks from your IT department. HR may also need to be involved, in order to weigh in on privacy policies and other security concerns. Think of this as an opportunity to get everyone together for a picnic.

DATA STORAGE

It's time to do a little bonding with your Security or Data Governance team. See what they have to say about the below questions. If your organization exists in multiple countries, provide prospective vendors with a list of your locations and ask them how they handle data storage in those countries. The proper handling of data has been a hot topic as of late, especially as it relates to GDPR regulations, so many vendors will be able to provide in-depth information regarding how they store data.

#314 If the LMS vendor will store your organization's data, what data storage guarantee does the vendor offer?

#315 Does your organization want to store all LMS data on a local (company) server for security purposes? Will the vendor allow this?

#316 If the vendor is cloud-based and your organization has European locations, does the vendor have a data storage facility in Europe? Research GDPR regulations and how they may affect your industry.

#317 If the vendor is cloud-based, where are the servers located?

#318 Does the vendor allow you to choose between an MS SQL or ODBC database? Does your IT department have a preference?

#319 Are copies of your data stored in multiple locations? Ask your LMS vendor for their redundancy plan.

#320 Where does course content need to be stored for the LMS to access it?

#321 Is data archiving available for all LMS data, such as courses, curricula, assessments, and user accounts?

#322 If you have security concerns, does the vendor support data encryption? In what ways?

#323 Ask the vendor to explain their system's data exchanges.

#324 Can data be exported into multiple formats? If you change learning management systems later, you will need to export data from your current LMS into the new system.

#325 Can your organization's current LMS data be imported easily?

#326 Can data be imported from common document types, such as those created in Microsoft Word or Excel?

#327   Can you import and export using batch files?

#328   Does your organization have additional criteria?

SYSTEM MAINTENANCE

Every learning management system requires ongoing updates and maintenance. It's good to know how much of an impact these activities will have on your organization. For example, a cloud-based LMS may be updated on a continuous basis with minimal involvement from your team. An on-premise platform (meaning one that is stored on your organization's servers) may require more involvement from your internal team when it's time for an update or upgrade. You can expect some periods of scheduled downtime regardless of what vendor you choose.

#329   How much involvement will your organization have during routine system updates and major upgrades?

#330   When do updates and upgrades occur?

#331   How much notice does the vendor provide?

#332   How long will it take the vendor to resolve routine issues? What support guarantees does the vendor offer as part of their Service Level Agreement (SLA)?

#333   Is the LMS usable in all browsers?

#334   Are browser plug-ins required for some LMS features?

#335   Does the LMS require Java?

#336   Does the LMS require ActiveX?

#337   What is the minimum Internet speed required for the LMS to load smoothly?

#338   Does your organization have additional criteria?

SECURITY & AUTHENTICATION

Here are more questions for your Security team! While they're weighing in, consider what experience you want the learner to have when they log onto the LMS. If your IT department can enable single sign-on (SSO), your learners won't have a separate log-on or password for the LMS. Once the learner logs onto their computer with, say, their Windows username and password, their identity is known. When the learner launches the LMS, they are automatically logged on using the details from their prior authentication. Assuming your users use dedicated devices rather than shared devices, SSO is a great way to make logging onto the LMS as fast as possible.

If you have questions, check out Learn Tech Collective's private LinkedIn group. Instructions to join can be found in the front of the book.

#339 What level of privacy does your organization guarantee to employees or students? Does the LMS conform to that level of privacy?

#340 How does the LMS vendor protect confidential data stored inside the LMS?

#341 If the LMS is transmitting data to other systems in your organization, how does the LMS assist in protecting transmitted data?

#342 Does your organization's IT department want an internal network installation? Will the LMS vendor accommodate this?

#343 If your IT department has standards for server-level user authentication, have the LMS vendor discuss with them.

#344 Will users be automatically logged onto the LMS using single sign-on (SSO)? This is something to discuss with your IT department.

#345 Can security settings be configured for manually entered passwords? For example, can you require a password to be over six characters long?

#346 Does the LMS force users to change their password from a generic password to a personalized password upon first log-on?

#347 Can database transactions be audited by an LMS administrator?

#348 Can audit logs be specified for desired database tables? (Have your IT department weigh in on whether this is needed.)

#349 Are before and after images logged for each database transaction?

#350 Does your organization have additional criteria?

8

MAKING THE LMS FRIENDLIER FOR ALL

A learning management system can and should be accessible to everyone in your organization, regardless of special needs or language requirements. Talk with HR and see what modifications the LMS may need in order to be usable by everyone. If you have an LMS steering committee, be sure the committee includes members who can speak to the needs of all of your learners. The more, the merrier.

ACCESSIBILITY

It's time to socialize with your HR team and legal counsel. Learning technology should accommodate the needs of everyone within your organization, both because you have the legal obligation to be accommodating, and because it's the right thing to do. HR will be able to help you understand the accessibility needs of your organization, and legal counsel can advise on what you should do to accommodate those needs.

#351   Is the LMS interface compliant with ADA Section 508? (Have your HR department define your organization's responsibilities.)

#352   Does the LMS support the use of screen readers?

#353   Are there tools that assist in adding captions to courses and assessments?

#354   Is it easy to add audio or video to course elements?

#355   Can users complete an assignment using alternative methods, such as submitting an audio file or video instead of a text document?

#356 Is it possible to increase the duration of assessments if certain users require more time?

#357 Does your organization have additional criteria?

SUPPORTING MULTIPLE LANGUAGES

Depending on your organization's diversity, you may want to make your LMS interface available in multiple languages. Keep in mind, however, that you can't magically change the language of the actual learning content, only the LMS interface. And be aware that having a platform available in multiple languages can make it more difficult for your administrators to deliver technical support.

#358 If your organization delivers the same course in multiple languages, how does an end user choose his/her preferred language?

#359 Is there a separate course catalog for each language?

#360 Is there a separate user interface for each language?

#361 Does the LMS support languages with multi-byte character sets, such as Chinese, Korean, and Japanese?

#362 Languages frequently required by international companies include: English, Spanish (Latin America), Spanish, German, French, French (Canadian), Dutch, Portuguese, Portuguese (Brazil), Hindi, Chinese, Korean, Japanese, Russian, and Arabic

#363 Does your organization have additional criteria?

MULTI-TENANT (MULTIPLE PORTALS)

What's more fun than one LMS? Lots of LMSs! A multi-tenant solution allows you to silo your platform so that you can have mutually exclusive groups all using the same system.

#364   If your organization is divided into multiple segments, or if you have multiple clients who will access LMS content, does the LMS vendor accommodate a multi-tenant set-up?

#365   Can your organization build multiple custom domains for different institutions or business units, with unique branding for each?

#366   Is data for each domain segmented, so that administrators for a domain only see data for that domain?

#367   Is it possible for a super administrator to make changes to, or report upon, all domains at once?

#368   Does your organization have additional criteria?

ECOMMERCE

Who wouldn't want to charge their learners to attend class? Granted, if the training you offer is for your internal employees only, getting them to pay you might be a little tricky. But if you teach learners who are external to your organization, you will probably appreciate the e-commerce features some learning management systems offer.

#369   Does the LMS support integrated e-commerce, so that you can sell course content?

#370   Can users buy a course using PayPal, a credit card, and/or other forms of online payment?

#371   How easy is it to complete a transaction using the system's shopping cart?

#372   Does the LMS use VeriSign or another cybersecurity software to ensure transaction security?

#373   How easily can a user apply a discount code during checkout?

#374 Is it possible to package a group of courses and sell them as a single product?

#375 Can prices be displayed for multiple currencies?

#376 Can the user specify a preferred currency?

#377 How robust are the e-commerce reporting features? Can you track payments, royalties, and charge-backs?

#378 Does your organization have additional criteria?

9

TRANSITIONING TO A NEW SYSTEM

Here we are at the last chapter. You're probably asking vendors some deep, insightful questions. And they're probably admiring how thorough you are... or at least they're tolerating it!

This is a good time to contemplate next steps. How easy will it be to jump from your existing LMS, if you have one, to the new LMS? And how much cash is your organization going to shell out? How much negotiating room do you have?

TRANSITIONING TO THE NEW LMS

It's almost time for the implementation! Make sure you know what to expect from your LMS vendor, and what they expect from you. Running an implementation requires cooperation from both sides. Check out YouTube channel Learn Tech Collective for more advice regarding LMS implementations.

#379 Will the vendor assign a specific representative to work with your organization? If your needs are complex, it's often better to communicate with one point-person.

#380 How easy is it to upload all courses and associated learning histories from your organization's current LMS?

#381 How are new users added to the LMS? Will new user accounts be automatically created using information from your organization's HRIS? Will you create new user accounts manually?

#382 If the LMS needs to communicate with other systems in your organization, can the LMS accept data from those systems? Can it communicate data to those systems? The LMS vendor may refer to this communication of data as "running a feed" between the systems.

#383   Does your organization have additional criteria?

CONTRACT CONSIDERATIONS

Before you sign a contract, have your LMS vendor break out all costs associated with the implementation and maintenance of your LMS. Are there any features or services you don't need? Say so. This is the easiest way to reduce the overall cost of your learning management system. Check out YouTube channel Learn Tech Collective for more negotiation advice.

#384   Will the vendor provide a free trial or "sandbox" of the LMS for your organization?

#385   What is the first-year price for the LMS? The cost of your first year is often significantly higher than subsequent years. This is because most vendors charge an implementation fee.

#386   What is the price for all subsequent years?

#387   How long is the contract?

#388   Does the vendor offer any assurance that the overall cost of your LMS will not inflate when it is time to renew? If you have concerns, you may want to contact some organizations currently using your vendor's LMS.

#389   If the number of employees in your organization increases or decreases, will the cost of your LMS change? Some vendors have a per-user licensing fee.

#390   Is training included in the initial contract price?

#391   Is support included in the initial contract price?

#392   If the LMS will be customized to meet your organization's needs, are the customization projects included in the contract price?

#393 If your organization will be accessing the LMS through mobile devices, is there an additional cost for mobile client access?

#394 Does your organization have additional criteria?

THAT'S ALL, FOLKS!

THANK YOU FOR READING!

IF YOU LEARNED SOMETHING FROM THIS BOOK, PLEASE HELP OTHERS FIND IT BY RATING IT ON **AMAZON.COM** OR DISCUSSING IT ON OUR SOCIAL MEDIA PAGES.

www.facebook.com/rofl411

www.twitter.com/rofl411

www.youtube.com/learntechcollective

HOPE TO HEAR FROM YOU SOON!

- KAT

SUPPORTERS

My most sincere thanks to the following individuals who contributed a combined total of $4,883 to support the republishing of this book, along with *LMS Success!* I appreciate your support of my work, and I hope you enjoy the finished product!

Sandra Cutler

Kevin Gumienny

Gene Idol

Adib Masumian

Heather Poggi-Mannis

Kent Russell

Matthew Sime

Renee Sopeta

Donald Twining

Karin Zijlstra

...and a few anonymous donors

ABOUT THE AUTHOR

Katrina Marie Baker owns Resources of Fun Learning, a learning and development publishing and consulting firm. Her clients range from Fortune 100 companies to small businesses. Katrina has also worked in global training capacities for a Fortune 500 retailer and two of the world's most prestigious law firms. In addition to this book, Katrina has authored *LMS Success!* and *Corporate Training Tips & Tricks*.

Katrina is a former Director of Technology with the Association for Talent Development, and she speaks at national and international events on LMS and e-learning topics. She has implemented over 25 learning management systems and mentored top-tier executives in the aerospace, legal, retail, and technology industries.

www.linkedin.com/in/katrinabaker

Made in the USA
Middletown, DE
30 November 2020

25715761R00060